LifeChange

S E R I E S

A life-changing encounter
with God's Word from the book of

1&2 KINGS

NAVPRESS

Discipleship Inside Out™

NavPress is the publishing ministry of The Navigators, an international Christian organization and leader in personal spiritual development. NavPress is committed to helping people grow spiritually and enjoy lives of meaning and hope through personal and group resources that are biblically rooted, culturally relevant, and highly practical.

For a free catalog go to www.NavPress.com
or call 1.800.366.7788 in the United States or 1.800.839.4769 in Canada.

ISBN: 978-1-61521-641-3

Printed in the United States of America

1 2 3 4 5 6 7 8 / 14 13 12 11

CONTENTS

HOW TO USE THIS STUDY

Although the LIFECHANGE guides vary with the individual books they explore, they share some common goals:

1. To provide you with a firm foundation of understanding and a thirst to return to the book

2. To give you study patterns and skills that help you explore every part of the Bible

3. To offer you historical background, word definitions, and explanation notes to aid your study

4. To help you grasp the message of the book as a whole

5. To teach you how to let God's Word transform you into Christ's image

As You Begin

This guide includes eight lessons, which will take you chapter by chapter through all of 1 and 2 Kings.

Each lesson is designed to take from one to two hours of preparation to complete on your own. To benefit most from this time, here's a good way to begin your work on each lesson:

1. Pray for God's help to keep you mentally alert and spiritually sensitive.

2. Read attentively through the entire passage mentioned in the lesson's title. (You may want to read the passage from two or more Bible versions, perhaps at least once from a more literal translation such as the New International Version, English Standard Version, New American Standard Bible, or New King James Version and perhaps once more in a paraphrase such as the New Living Translation.) Do your reading in an environment that's as free as possible from distractions. Allow your mind and heart to meditate on these words you encounter, words that are God's personal gift to you and all His people.

After reading the passage, you're ready to dive into the numbered questions in this guide, which make up the main portion of each lesson. Each of these questions is followed by blank space for writing your answers. (This act of writing your answers helps clarify your thinking and stimulates your mental engagement with the passage as well as your later recall.) Use extra paper or a notebook if the space for recording your answers seems too small. Continue through the questions in numbered order. If any question seems too difficult or unclear, just skip it and go on to the next.

Each of these questions will typically direct back to 1 and 2 Kings to look again at a certain portion of the assigned passage for that lesson. (At this point, be sure to use a more literal Bible translation rather than a paraphrase.)

As you look closer at the questions and passages, it's helpful to approach them in this progression:

Observe. What does the passage actually *say*? Ask God to help you see it clearly. Notice everything that's there.

Interpret. What does the passage *mean*? Ask God to help you understand. And remember that any passage's meaning is fundamentally determined by its *context*. Stay alert to all you'll see about the setting and background of 1 and 2 Kings, and keep thinking of these books as a whole while you proceed through them chapter by chapter. You'll be progressively building up your insights and familiarity with what they're all about.

Apply. Keep asking yourself, *How does this truth affect my life?* (Pray for God's help as you examine yourself in light of that truth and in light of His purpose for each passage.)

Try to consciously follow all three of these approaches as you shape your written answer to each question in the lesson.

The Extras

In addition to the regular numbered questions you see in this guide, each lesson also offers several "optional" questions or suggestions that appear in the margins. All of these will appear under one of three headings:

Optional Application. Try as many of these questions as you can without overcommitting yourself, considering them with prayerful sensitivity to the Lord's guidance.

For Thought and Discussion. Many of these questions address various ethical issues and other biblical principles that lead to a wide range of implications. They tend to be particularly suited for group discussions.

For Further Study. These often include cross-references to other parts of the Bible that shed light on a topic in the lesson, plus questions that delve deeper into the passage.

(For additional help for more effective Bible study, refer to the "Study Aids" section on page 91.)

Changing Your Life

Don't let your study become an exercise in knowledge alone. Treat the passage as God's Word, and stay in dialogue with Him as you study. Pray, "Lord, what do You want me to notice here?" "Father, why is this true?" "Lord, how does my life measure up to this?"

Let biblical truth sink into your inner convictions so you'll increasingly be able to act on this truth as a natural way of living.

At times you may want to consider memorizing a certain verse or passage you come across in your study, one that particularly challenges or encourages you. To help with that, write down the words on a card to keep with you, and set aside a few minutes each day to think about the passage. Recite it to yourself repeatedly, always thinking about its meaning. Return to it as often as you can, for a brief review. You'll soon find the words coming to mind spontaneously, and they'll begin to affect your motives and actions.

For Group Study

Exploring Scripture together in a group is especially valuable for the encouragement, support, and accountability it provides as you seek to apply God's Word to your life. Together you can listen jointly for God's guidance, pray for each other, help one another resist temptation, and share the spiritual principles you're learning to put into practice. Together you affirm that growing in faith, hope, and love is important and that you need each other in the process.

A group of four to ten people allows for the closest understanding of each other and the richest discussions in Bible study, but you can adapt this guide for other-sized groups. It will suit a wide range of group types, such as home Bible studies, growth groups, youth groups, and church classes. Both new and mature Christians will benefit from the guide, regardless of their previous experience in Bible study.

Aim for a positive atmosphere of acceptance, honesty, and openness. In your first meeting, explore candidly everyone's expectations and goals for your time together.

A typical schedule for group study is to take one lesson per week, but feel free to split lessons if you want to discuss them more thoroughly. Or omit some questions in a lesson if your preparation or discussion time is limited. (You can always return to this guide later for further study on your own.)

When you come together, you probably won't have time to discuss all the questions in the lesson, so it's helpful to choose ahead of time the ones you want to make sure to cover thoroughly. This is one of the main responsibilities that a group leader typically assumes.

Each lesson in this guide ends with a section called "For the Group." It gives advice for that particular lesson on how to focus the discussion, how to apply the lesson to daily life, and so on. Reading each lesson's "For the Group" section ahead of time can help the leader be more effective in guiding the group.

You'll get the greatest benefit from your time together if each group member also prepares ahead of time by writing out his or her answers to each question in the lesson. The private reflection and prayer that this preparation can stimulate will be especially important in helping everyone discern how God wants you to apply each lesson to your daily life.

There are many ways to structure the group meeting, and in fact you may want to vary your routine occasionally to help keep things fresh.

Here are some of the elements you can consider including as you come together for each lesson:

Pray together. It's good to pause for prayer as you begin your time together. When you begin with prayer, it's worthwhile and honoring to God to ask especially for His Holy Spirit's guidance of your time together. If you write down each other's prayer requests, you are more likely to remember to pray for them during the week, ask about them at the next meeting, and notice answered prayers. You might want to get a notebook for prayer requests and discussion notes.

Worship. Some groups like to sing together and worship God with prayers of praise.

Review. You may want to take time to discuss what difference the previous week's lesson has made in your life as well as recall the major emphasis you discovered in the passage for that week.

Read the passage aloud. Once you're ready to focus attention together on the assigned Scripture passage in the week's lesson, read it aloud. (One person could do this, or the reading could be shared.)

Open up for lingering questions. Allow time for the group members to mention anything in the passage that they may have particular questions about.

Summarize the passage. Have one or two people offer a summary of what the passage tells about.

Discuss. This will be the heart of your time together and will likely take the biggest portion of your time. Focus on the questions you see as the most important and most helpful. Allow and encourage everyone to be part of the discussion for each question. You may want to take written notes as the discussion proceeds. Ask follow-up questions to sharpen your attention and deepen your understanding of what you discuss. You may want to give special attention to the questions in the margin under the heading "For Thought and Discussion."

Encourage further personal study. You can find more opportunities for exploring the lesson's themes and issues under the marginal heading "For Further Study" throughout the lesson. You can also pursue some of these together during your group time.

Focus on application. Look especially at the "Optional Application" sections found in the margins. Keep encouraging one another in the continual work of adjusting your lives to the truths God gives in Scripture.

Summarize your discoveries. You may want to read aloud through the passage one last time together, using the opportunity to solidify your understanding and appreciation of it and to clarify how the Lord is speaking to you through it.

Look ahead. Glance together at the headings and questions in the next
  lesson to see what's coming next.

Give thanks to God. It's good to end your time together by pausing to express
  gratitude to God for His Word and for the work of His Spirit in your
  minds and hearts during your time together.

THE BOOKS OF KINGS

An End (and a Beginning)

The books of 1 and 2 Kings dive immediately into a continuation of the dramatic story told in 1 and 2 Samuel—a story that centered on the prophet Samuel and his anointing of Israel's first two kings (Saul and David) and gave a gripping account of their long, tumultuous reigns.

Now, as 1 Kings opens, David is an old man nearing death, and the narrative quickly focuses on conflict and conspiracy regarding the rightful succession to his throne. It's a shaky situation that gives the reader pause. Will the highest promises of David's reign lead now to even greater things? Will David's line yield more men "after God's own heart"? Will they be good shepherds to guide Israel into a triumphant and ever-expanding fulfillment of the God-exalting, world-reaching, heart-transforming truths David sang about?

Or will our hearts be sickened by hope deferred?

The books of Kings will tell us.

A Clear Account

Originally, these two books of Kings were by all indications a single work that was later divided in half for convenience. Both parts reflect the same theme, tone, language, and purpose. "Kings bears the impress of being a unified book expressing the viewpoint of a single author who has woven together his historical data in accordance with a single purpose and with a uniform literary style."[1]

Some scholars believe that 1 and 2 Kings may well have been composed by the same author or authors who wrote Joshua, Judges, and 1 and 2 Samuel. (In some traditions going back to ancient times, the two books of Samuel and the two books of Kings are presented as four parts of the same work.) Although the scholarly speculations about this are fascinating, the books themselves provide no clear indication of who their author is. Fortunately, identifying that author is unnecessary for understanding and thoroughly appreciating their content.

Taken together, the text of 1 and 2 Kings has about the same number of words as the combined books of Samuel or the combined books of 1 and 2 Chronicles. Each of these three combined works—Samuel, Kings, and

Chronicles—is only slightly shorter than the book of Jeremiah, the longest of all the Bible's books (in terms of total words). So in sheer size alone, the combined work of 1 and 2 Kings commands a prominent place in the Old Testament and in all of Scripture.

In general, the events described in 1 and 2 Kings are narrated chronologically, although there's a little jumping back and forth in time after Israel splits into two kingdoms (see 1 Kings 12), at which point the author begins telling the separate stories of the two kingdoms by alternating from one to the other.

Eventually, the histories of both kingdoms will end tragically, each with its capital besieged and conquered and its people taken captive by the prevailing foreign power at the time. The northern kingdom of Israel will fall to the Assyrian empire late in the eighth century BC; the southern kingdom of Judah will then fall to the Babylonian (Chaldean) empire early in the sixth century.

Given this basic chronological progression in the narrative, perhaps the simplest outline of the combined books of Kings is to see three major parts:

1. Solomon's reign over all Israel, before the kingdom splits in two (1 Kings 1–11)
2. The separate kingdoms of Judah and Israel in their side-by-side existence, a situation lasting until Israel goes into exile (1 Kings 12–2 Kings 17)
3. Judah existing alone until she, too, goes into exile (2 Kings 18–25)

Part 2 above is the longest (representing twenty-six chapters, compared to eleven in the first part and eight in the third). So that longer second part might also be further sectioned in various ways in an outline. For gaining a better overview of Kings, you may find it helpful to carefully outline this long middle section on your own. You could further divide it according to each of the kings as their successive stories are told as well as perhaps identify various stages in the story of the prophets Elijah and Elisha.

Interestingly, the amount of space devoted in 1 and 2 Kings to each ruler's reign varies widely, and the differences don't correspond to the actual length of their time on the throne. Also, the pace of the narrative accelerates at times, with decades racing by in a few sentences or paragraphs, and then slows down to concentrate a number of pages on a few certain events and individuals.

A Tragic Climax to an Epic Story

As already mentioned, the story told in 1 and 2 Kings appears quite closely related to the long narrative of earlier events presented in the books of Joshua, Judges, and 1 and 2 Samuel. And the book of Joshua, of course, is clearly a continuation of the vast story told in the Torah, the Bible's first five books. All of the Bible from Genesis through 2 Kings can thus be viewed as one single story, vast and sweeping and many-sided yet clearly unified in theme and direction.

In comparison to this immense story, what comes immediately after 2 Kings in our Bibles—the books of 1 and 2 Chronicles, Ezra, Nehemiah, and Esther—not only seems to reflect clearly different (and later) authorship traditions but also basically goes back over the ground already covered in the earlier books. From their own viewpoint and in their own style, the books retell the whole story all over again. (They also carry the narrative forward by unfolding certain important events in the century and a half that followed Judah's captivity.)

Meanwhile, the remainder of the Old Testament—from Job and Psalms on to the end—includes various literary works of worship and wisdom as well as the majestic and magisterial writings of the prophets who lived and spoke especially during the years described in 2 Kings and for a great many decades afterward.

In this wide scope of things, the book we know as 1 and 2 Kings therefore occupies a place in the story with built-in emphasis: It's at the "first" end, the initial wrap-up and climax of the great overarching history of a world created by God and of a particular people in it who were handpicked by God.

The ending we press forward to in the final pages of 2 Kings is devastatingly tragic—yet not utterly so, for in its necessary tragedy we find seeds of hope, the hints and promise of something better to come, all vitally linked to the character of the God who reveals Himself as this story's ultimate Author as well as its major "Character" (and the only one present in every scene).

As we understand it better, the inevitably tragic climax in 2 Kings that this gigantic story has been spiraling toward can't help but intensify what will unfold next. Our teary eyes will be ready to truly see it, our broken hearts ready to feel it, our numbed minds ready to be stirred awake by it. We'll find that the glory of "the story beyond the story" is ever more richly hinted at and prefigured and promised in the Old Testament prophets before it finally bursts forth with incomparable and unconquerable heat and light in the New Testament, racing toward a joyful-ever-after ending that is beyond all imagining.

Death and Life

The narrative points to Jesus in many ways as it moves beyond a mere historical record.

"Kings is . . . more than an account of the political and social history of this period. It records Israel's spiritual response to God who had taken her into covenant relationship with himself (2 Kings 17:7-23), and who had bestowed great privileges to her through the promise made to David (1 Kings 2:2-4). Accordingly, within its pages is found a detailed summary of the spiritual experiences of her people—particularly her kings, prophets, and priests, whose activities largely point to the need for the advent of the one who would combine the intended ideal of these three offices in himself."[2] The person who would manifest "in himself" this "intended ideal" is, of course, Jesus Christ.

Also pointing to Christ in Kings is how anything and everything else that might justify spiritual confidence—kingly wisdom, the temple, the law, national power, moral and religious reform—is shown to be ultimately ineffective.

This reflects the deeper prophetic message in 1 and 2 Kings: a matter of death and life. "The message of the prophets is not, 'Israel has sinned; therefore, Israel needs to get its act together or it will die.' The message is, 'Israel has sinned; therefore, Israel must die, and its only hope is to entrust itself to a God who will give it new life on the far side of death.' Or even, 'Israel has sinned; Israel is already dead. Cling to the God who raises the dead.' This is precisely the prophetic message of 1–2 Kings, which systematically dismantles Israel's confidence in everything but the omnipotent mercy and patience of God. . . . Ultimately, for a Christian reading, 1–2 Kings is prophetic because it points to, anticipates, and foreshadows the gospel of Jesus the Christ, and a Christian reading of 1–2 Kings must regard it not primarily as historical, prophetic, or sapiential but as evangelical."[3]

Timeline: The Rulers of Israel and Judah

In the following chart, approximate dates are given for each reign. Sometimes a king's reign would overlap that of his successor for a certain period.

Distinguishing between these rulers can be confusing because a king's name is often similar or identical to that of another king.

RULING OVER A UNITED ISRAEL
Saul (1050–1010 BC)
David (1010–970)
Solomon (970–930)

AFTER THE KINGDOM DIVIDED	
Ruling in Judah	Ruling in Israel
Rehoboam (930–914)	**Jeroboam I** (930–910)
Abijah [Abijam] (914–911)	
Asa (911–870)	**Nadab** (910–909)
	Baasha (909–886)
	Elah (886–885)
	Zimri (885)
	Tibni [rival to Omri] (885–880)
	Omri (885–874)
Jehoshaphat (870–848)	**Ahab** (874–853)
	Ahaziah (853–852)
Jehoram [Joram] (848–842)	**Joram** [Jehoram] (852–841)

Ahaziah (842–841)	Jehu (841–813)
Athaliah [queen] (841–835)	
Joash [Jehoash] (835–795)	Jehoahaz (813–797)
Amaziah (795–767)	Jehoash [Joash] (797–781)
Azariah [Uzziah] (767–739)	Jeroboam II (782–753)
	Zechariah (753–752)
	Shallum (752)
	Menahem (752–741)
	Pekahiah (741–739)
Jotham (750–730)	Pekah (739–731)
Ahaz (730–715)	Hoshea (731–722)
	(ISRAEL FALLS TO ASSYRIA: 722 BC)
Hezekiah (715–686)	
Manasseh (686–642)	
Amon (642–640)	
Josiah (640–609)	
Jehoahaz (609)	
Jehoiakim (609–598)	
Jehoiachin (598–597)	
Zedekiah (597–586)	
(JUDAH FALLS TO BABYLON: 586 BC)	

1. Richard D. Patterson and Hermann J. Austel, *1, 2 Kings*, vol. 4 in THE EXPOSITOR'S BIBLE COMMENTARY, ed. Frank E. Gaebelein (Grand Rapids, MI: Zondervan, 1988), 5.
2. Patterson and Austel, 4.
3. Peter J. Leithart, *1 and 2 Kings* (Grand Rapids, MI: Baker, 2006), 18, 20.

1 KINGS 1–4

In David's Shadow

*The eyes of all Israel are on you, to learn from
you who will sit on the throne.*

1 KINGS 1:20

1. For getting the most from 1 and 2 Kings, one
of the best guidelines is found in 2 Timothy
3:16-17, words Paul wrote with the Old Testament first in view. He said that *all* Scripture is
of great benefit to teach us, rebuke us, correct
us, and train us in righteousness. Paul added
that these Scriptures completely equip the person of God "for every good work." As you think
seriously about those guidelines, in which of
these areas do you especially want to experience
the usefulness of 1 and 2 Kings? Express your
desire in a written prayer to God.

_____

_____

_____

_____

2. In Jeremiah 23:29, God says that His Word is
like fire and like a hammer. He can use the
Scriptures to burn away unclean thoughts and
desires in our hearts. He can also use Scripture,
with hammer-like hardness, to crush and
crumble our spiritual hardness. From your
study of these books of Kings, how do you most

For Thought and Discussion: Look over passages focusing on the prophets in 1 and 2 Kings, as listed in the shaded box on the next page. What typical kinds of work does God give the prophets to do? What do these prophets have in common?

want to see the "fire and hammer" power of God's Word at work in your own life? Again, express this longing in a written prayer to God.

_____

_____

_____

_____

3. Glance ahead through the pages of 1 Kings, looking for a recurring theme or thought in each of the following verses: 2:4, 8:23, 8:48, 11:4, 14:8, 15:3, and 15:14. (And in the book of 2 Kings, notice it again in these verses: 10:31, 20:3, 23:3, and 23:25.) What is that theme? Why is it important to God, and why is it important for all of God's people in all ages?

_____

_____

_____

_____

4. As you read attentively through the opening four chapters of 1 Kings, how would you assess the strengths and weaknesses of the kingdom of Israel at this time?

_____

_____

_____

5. In the first chapter of 1 Kings, what human motivations and emotions are particularly prominent in the main characters?

_____

_____

_____

6. After reading the story of Adonijah, what similarities do you see between it and the earlier
story of Adonijah's brother Absalom (see especially 2 Samuel 14:25; 15:1-12)?

_____

_____

_____

Optional
Application: What
good counsel do
you find for yourself
in David's words to
Solomon in 2:2-3?

7. What are the most important factors you see
   behind Adonijah's failure—and Solomon's
   success—in securing succession to their father
   David's throne?

   _____

   _____

   _____

   _____

"Because he works out political theology in narrative form, the author of 1–2
Kings displays a Shakespearean sense of
the interplay of public and private, rec-
ognizing that great public events often
arise from intimate and tenuous private
concerns."[2]

8. In 2:2-3, David gives instructions to his son
   Solomon, Israel's new king. Compare these words
   to those spoken by God to Israel's new leader in
   Joshua 1:6-9 (see also Deuteronomy 31:1-8).

   a. What similarities do you see in these two sets
      of instructions?

      _____

      _____

      _____

   b. How were Solomon's and Joshua's circum-
      stances significantly similar, and how were
      they significantly different?

      _____

      _____

      _____

20

9. In 2:4, David apparently refers to words God spoke to him earlier through the prophet Nathan. Look back at these words in 2 Samuel 7:8-16 and summarize their continuing importance for Solomon and for all the kings of Israel to come.

_____

_____

_____

For Further Study: For background on the three men David gives Solomon instructions about in 2:5-9, see especially 2 Samuel 3:22-32, 16:5-13, 19:31-39, and 20:7-10.

10. As David's life comes to a close, what strengths and weaknesses can you identify in his leadership, as evidenced in these first two chapters of 1 Kings?

_____

_____

_____

11. David is known in Scripture as a man after God's own heart (see 1 Samuel 13:14; Acts 13:22). From the evidence you see in 1 Kings 1 and 2, does that still seem to be true of him in his old age?

_____

_____

_____

As the Lord lives (1:29). This solemn oath is used more than a dozen times in 1 and 2 Kings and appears more than thirty times in the Bible's historical books (in Judges through Chronicles). It's also common in the book of Jeremiah.

12. In 1:48 and 2:15, notice that both David and his son Adonijah acknowledge that Solomon's succession to the throne was brought about by God Himself. In what primary ways do you think this fact has become obvious to each of them?

_____

Optional Application: If God presented you with the question He gave Solomon in 3:5—if He invited you to ask Him for anything you wanted—what would you ask for?

For Thought and Discussion: How would you define *wisdom* in the truest biblical sense?

13. In chapter 3, what is revealed about God's character in what He relates to Solomon and the manner in which He does it?

_____

_____

_____

_____

High places (3:3). "The idea is simply that of publicly accessible structures (including unenclosed altars and temples with altars) within which or on which offerings were made to God or the gods. The continuation and proliferation of these local places of worship (as opposed to the one place of worship described in Deuteronomy 12) is one of the main concerns of the authors of 1–2 Kings."[3] (See 1 Kings 12:31; 22:43; 2 Kings 12:3; 14:4; 15:4,35; 16:4; 21:3.)

14. In 3:6-9, analyze carefully the various reasons Solomon gives for his request in response to God's invitation. What do these things tell you about Solomon the man?

_____

_____

_____

15. As Solomon's reign proceeds, how well does he make use of the wisdom God has given him? (Indicate the passages that shape your answer.)

_____

_____

_____

22

People . . . as numerous as the sand on the seashore (4:20). This is the first time in Scripture that this phrase is used to describe what Israel has become. Always before the phrase was simply a promise of what Israel would be in the future (see God's promise to Abraham in Genesis 22:17-18 and to Jacob in 32:12).

From the River to the land of the Philistines, as far as the border of Egypt (4:21). Solomon's kingdom has spread out to the extent promised to Abraham (see Genesis 15:18) and to Moses and the Israelites (see Exodus 23:31).

16. How do Solomon's accomplishments in 4:33 reflect a fulfillment of God's purpose for mankind as stated in Genesis 1:28?

_____

_____

_____

17. What conclusions would you make in these chapters about Solomon's spiritual life? (Indicate the passages that shape your answer.)

_____

_____

_____

18. What would you select as the key verse or passage in 1 Kings 1–4—the passage that best captures or reflects the dynamics of what these chapters are all about?

_____

_____

19. List any lingering questions you have about 1 Kings 1–4.

_____

_____

_____

For Thought and Discussion: What do you consider to be the most important traits of good leadership, and how do these compare with what you see in the opening chapters of 1 Kings?

For the Group

In your first meeting, it may be helpful to turn to the front of this book and review together the "How to Use This Study" section.

You may want to focus your discussion for lesson 1 on the following issues, themes, and concepts. (These things will likely reflect what group members have learned in their individual study of this week's passage, although they'll also have made discoveries in other areas as well.)

- God's faithfulness to His promises
- Our proper involvement in government and politics and the issues and complexities involved with that
- Decisiveness when faced with hard choices

The following numbered questions in lesson 1 may stimulate your best and most helpful discussion: 4, 5, 7, 8, 13, and 15.

Look also at the questions in the margin under the heading "For Thought and Discussion."

1. Paul R. House, *1, 2 Kings*, vol. 8 in New American Commentary, ed. E. Ray Clendenen (Nashville: Broadman, Holman, 1995), 57.
2. Peter J. Leithart, *1 and 2 Kings* (Grand Rapids, MI: Baker, 2006), 35.
3. *ESV Study Bible* (Wheaton, IL: Crossway, 2008), on 1 Kings 3:3.

1 KINGS 5–8

Solomon's Glory

Building of the temple Ch. 5+6

1 Kings 6:1-14 The creative Act

Praying in Your Own words

1 Kings 8:38-40

I intend, therefore, to build a temple for the Name of the LORD my God.

1 KINGS 5:5

1. After reading 1 Kings 5–8, assess Solomon's leadership from the evidence you see here. Where was he strong, and where was he weak?

_____

_____

_____

2. In chapters 5–8, what is significant about so many details being given for the design and construction of the temple and its furnishings? How might such a comprehensive description have affected this book's original readers?

_____

_____

_____

For Further Study: Compare the quantity of details given in 1 Kings 6–8 about the temple's construction with the lengthy narratives on making the tabernacle (see Exodus 25–40) and the detailed description of Ezekiel's envisioned temple (see Ezekiel 40–48). Why are these things important enough to be given such attention in Scripture? And what might this have to say about the body of Christ as the new temple of God? Explore 1 Corinthians 3:16, 2 Corinthians 6:16, Ephesians 2:22, 1 Timothy 3:15, and 1 Peter 2:5.

Tabernacle and Temple

In the book of Exodus, after the people of Israel left Egypt, God had commanded the construction of a portable tent sanctuary known as the tabernacle: "Have them make a sanctuary for me, and I will dwell among them" (Exodus 25:8). Most of the second half of Exodus is taken up with the specific plans and details of erecting and furnishing this tabernacle.

Later, in Deuteronomy 12:5-6, Moses tells the Israelites, "You shall seek *the place* that the LORD your God will choose out of all your tribes to put his name and make his habitation there. There you shall go, and there you shall bring your burnt offerings and your sacrifices, your tithes and the contribution that you present, your vow offerings, your freewill offerings, and the firstborn of your herd and of your flock" (ESV, emphasis added). By God's guidance through the centuries, His people came to understand that this "place" was Jerusalem, the city David chose and built up as the capital of his kingdom.

The tabernacle, along with the ark it contained, had wound up in various places over the years (including captivity by the Philistines—see 1 Samuel 4:1-11). But now that David's capital city was established, he felt ready to build a permanent temple that would house the ark and replace the tabernacle as God's dwelling place among His people.

When David expressed this desire and received prophetic encouragement for it (see 2 Samuel 7:1-3), God responded that very night with one of the richest prophetic messages in all of Scripture. (Read it in 2 Samuel 7:4-17 along with the prayer in 7:18-29 that David, humbled and overwhelmed, offered in response.)

The substance of that prophecy to David informs and enriches the meaning of the actual construction building and dedication of the temple by Solomon, David's son.

3. As you are able to envision it, what aspects of the temple's architecture strike you as particularly pleasing or appealing to the eye?

_____

4. Does the building of the temple represent Solomon's greatest accomplishment? Why or why not?

_____

_____

_____

5. Read 1 Kings 6:12-13, words from the Lord directed at Solomon. As king, what are his specific responsibilities and what impact will his faithfulness (or lack of it) have for the entire nation?

_____

_____

_____

6. In what particular ways would you say the temple reflects the personality and character of God?

_____

_____

_____

7. Chapter 8 focuses first on the ark and its inclusion in the new temple. Look back to 1 Samuel 4–6 and in 2 Samuel 6 to review the dramatic circumstances surrounding the ark in previous generations. Summarize these things and tell how this story is brought to completion here in 1 Kings 8:1-9.

_____

_____

_____

_____

_____

For Further Study: Compare the description here of the temple's innermost room (see 6:16 and 6:23-28) with the same inner room in the tabernacle built by Moses (see Exodus 26:33-34) and in the temple Ezekiel saw in his vision from God (see Ezekiel 41:3-4; 41:21-23). What similarities do you see, and what differences? Also, review Hebrews 9:3-9 and 10:19-22 to see how God's people today are to view this innermost room in God's dwelling place.

For Further Study: Compare 8:6-9 (about the ark taken into the new temple) with the Lord's prophetic words about the ark in Jeremiah 3:16-18 and with what John sees in Revelation 11:19. How do these descriptions all fit together?

For Further Study:
Compare what happens in the temple in 1 Kings 8:10-11 with what happens in the tabernacle in Exodus 40:34-35 and in Ezekiel's envisioned temple in Ezekiel 43:1-5. Taken together, what do these passages mean today for us, who, in the church, "are the temple of the living God" (2 Corinthians 6:16)?

For Thought and Discussion:
Solomon's prayer repeatedly pleads for God to hear His people's prayers, wherever they are, and whatever their need (see 8:30-52). What can this teach us about the appropriate content of our prayers today?

For Further Study:
Solomon's temple dedication prayer (see 1 Kings 8:22-53) frequently echoes the book of Deuteronomy. As you look up the following verses, identify the place in Solomon's prayer where there seems to be a connection: Deuteronomy 3:24; 4:20,34-35,39; 5:15; 7:9; 9:26,29; 11:17; 12:1,11; 25:1; 28:21-22,37-38,42,45,52; 31:6,26.

8. What is the significance of what happens in 8:10-11?

_____

_____

_____

9. In 8:12-21, what appear to be the most important things Solomon understands about his heritage and responsibilities passed on to him from his father?

_____

_____

_____

10. In 8:22-53, how would you summarize the most significant requests Solomon makes of the Lord in his prayer for the dedication of the temple?

_____

_____

_____

11. What evidence do you find in Solomon's prayer that he especially understands the following attributes of God?

a. His love and faithfulness

_____

_____

b. His holiness and justice

_____

_____

c. His power

_____

_____

28

12. In what ways do Solomon's words to the people in 8:54-61 reflect timeless and universal longings, principles, and truths for how God's people worship Him?

_____

_____

_____

13. Look again at what the people did in 8:65-66. In what ways, and for what reasons, should something like this also be the experience of God's people today?

_____

_____

_____

14. What would you select as the key verse or passage in 1 Kings 5–8—the one that best captures or reflects the dynamics of what these chapters are all about?

_____

_____

15. List any lingering questions you have about 1 Kings 5–8.

_____

_____

_____

_____

Optional Application: Which statements and phrases in Solomon's prayer are especially good and timely as part of your own communication with God today?

For Further Study: In 8:60, Solomon was looking beyond the kingdom of Israel to the universal kingdom of God. How do his words about this compare with those of Joshua (see Joshua 4:23-24), David (see Psalm 86:8-10), Hezekiah (see Isaiah 37:18-20), and Isaiah (see Isaiah 52:10)?

For the Group

What truths, principles, and guidelines for worship can we glean from the details given here of this first temple built for the Lord in Jerusalem?

You may want to focus your discussion for lesson 2 on the following issues, themes, and concepts. (These things will likely reflect what group members have learned in their individual study of this week's passage, although they'll also have made discoveries in other areas as well.)

- Truths, principles, and guidelines regarding worship that pleases God
- Truths, principles, and guidelines regarding prayer that pleases God
- The miracle of God coming to dwell among humanity

The following numbered questions in lesson 2 may stimulate your best and most helpful discussion: 4, 5, 6, 10, and 12.

Look also at the questions in the margin under the heading "For Thought and Discussion."

1 KINGS 9–11

First Steps Downward

The LORD became angry with Solomon because his heart had turned away from the LORD, the God of Israel.

1 KINGS 11:9

1. Chapter 9 has been called the key to the book of 1 Kings. Why might this be so?

_____

_____

_____

2. From what you see in chapter 9, what is God's attitude toward this temple Solomon has built? And what promises does He make to Solomon?

_____

_____

_____

Optional Application: Review what God tells Solomon to do in 9:4. Can God require this also of you? Is He requiring it? If so, in what way? In what ways has Christ already fulfilled this requirement for you, and in what ways is He continuing to do so *in* and *through* you? What adjustments are needed now in your life so that you can better fulfill this requirement?

To this day (9:13). This phrase occurs frequently in 1 and 2 Kings, indicating a noticeable time interval between the occurrence of these events and the time when the book came together in its present form. (The phrase in Hebrew occurs also in 8:8; 10:12; and 12:19; and in 2 Kings 2:22; 8:22; 10:27; 14:7; 16:6; 17:23,34,41; and 21:15.)

For Further Study:
Compare what you read in 1 Kings about Solomon's wealth with the words of Jesus in Matthew 6:28-30. How did Jesus view the wealth and splendor of Solomon?

For Thought and Discussion: If you could go back in time and act as a royal adviser to King Solomon, what kind of counsel would you give him, and how and when would you express it?

3. In chapters 9–11, how well does Solomon continue to make use of the wisdom God has given him? (Indicate the passages that shape your answer.)

_____

_____

_____

4. Is Solomon's vast wealth (see especially 10:14-29, and also refer back to 4:22-28) meant to demonstrate to God's people that wealth is the reward for wisdom? Why or why not?

_____

_____

_____

5. Review the stipulations God gave to Moses in Deuteronomy 17:14-20 regarding a king in Israel. What is your best explanation for Solomon's blatant violation of some of these commands as we see in 1 Kings 10 and 11?

_____

_____

_____

"In the larger scheme of 1–2 Kings, Solomon's failure is nestled within a story of Israel's failure. Successful as he is, Solomon does not bring in a perpetual golden age. Human wisdom cannot bring in salvation for a fallen Israel or a fallen humanity. That can be done only through God's wisdom in flesh, a wisdom that confounds the wisdom of the wise, a wisdom that looks for all the world like folly."[1]

6. Do Solomon's actions reveal the shortcomings of his "wisdom"? Or did he ultimately depart from that wisdom? Explain your answer.

_____

_____

_____

7. In 1 Kings 11:6, we read that Solomon's actions were "evil in the eyes of the LORD." This phrase, first occurring here, will be used almost one hundred times in 1 and 2 Kings. Think carefully about each part of that phrase. What is the profound significance of it?

_____

_____

_____

8. What has Solomon lost as a result of his wrongdoing?

_____

_____

9. How are Solomon's particular sins reflective of our own sins today? Are there significant parallels?

_____

_____

_____

Optional Application: What do we *lose* when we, like Solomon, direct our devotion away from God and toward someone or something else instead? Acknowledge this in prayer to God, remembering to thank Him for His mercy to us in Christ, and to confess to Him any specific ways that you have recently turned away from Him.

Adversary (11:14,23,25). This word used to describe Solomon's foes Hadad and Rezon is the Hebrew word *satan*, the same as the name for the Devil (see also 1 Chronicles 21:1; Job 1:6-9; Matthew 4:10; Romans 16:20; 1 Peter 5:8).

Ahijah the prophet (11:29). From this point forward, almost to the end of 2 Kings, prophetic material and activity is mentioned in almost every chapter.

33

The book of the annals of Solomon (11:41). Other sources mentioned for the history in 1 and 2 Kings include "the book of the annals of the kings of Israel" (14:19, and mentioned sixteen other times in 1 and 2 Kings) and "the book of the annals of the kings of Judah" (14:29, and fourteen other times). These indicate a narrative that is carefully and conscientiously researched.

"To consider Kings as no more than history of the monarchy would strip the book of its theological value, since the author is not a dispassionate observer, merely chronicling his nation's past. Nevertheless, the historical value of his work should not be under-estimated. In composing a coherent and meaningful account of his nation's past, the biblical writer has provided an invaluable service to anyone who wants to understand this momentous era in Israelite history."[2]

10. Perhaps surprisingly, in telling us about Solomon's adversaries, the author of 1 Kings seems to tell about Hadad as a parallel to the story of Joseph and Moses, and about Rezon and Jeroboam as parallels to David's story. In what ways are their stories similar, and what might be the significance of these parallels?

a. Hadad similar to Joseph and Moses

_____

_____

_____

b. Rezon similar to David

_____

_____

_____

c. Jeroboam similar to David

_____

_____

_____

11. How would you describe and assess the development of Solomon's personal relationship with the Lord over the course of his reign?

_____

_____

_____

12. How would you describe Solomon's worst faults or character flaws?

_____

_____

13. Especially in chapter 11, how does God's response to Solomon reveal both His grace and His justice?

_____

_____

_____

"A careful reading of 1–2 Kings reveals a God who is always giving more than people ask, imagine, or deserve . . . a God of infinite, uncanny, unnerving patience."[3]

14. Review carefully the words of the Lord spoken to Jeroboam through the prophet Ahijah in 11:29-39. What do these words disclose about God's standards for both His people and the

ruler of His people, as well as His commitment to them?

_____

_____

_____

A lamp for David (11:36). In this verse, God promises that David will "always have a lamp before me in Jerusalem." (Look ahead to where this particular "lamp" is mentioned again in 1 Kings 15:4 and 2 Kings 8:19; see also its earlier mention in 2 Samuel 21:17.) "The Davidic flame will always burn."[4] A lamp in Scripture often represents something living (such as a person's life—see, for example, Job 18:6), and the extinguishing of that lamp represents its death. In Psalm 132:17, God makes this promise: "Here I will make a horn grow for David and set up a lamp for my anointed one."

15. Go back and look at the desires expressed for Solomon's reign in 1:37 and 1:47. How would you assess the degree to which these desires were actually fulfilled?

_____

_____

_____

16. What are the most important things we learn about Jeroboam in chapter 11?

_____

_____

17. What are the most important things that the prophet Ahijah communicates to Jeroboam in 11:30-39?

_____

_____

18. What would you select as the key verse or passage in 1 Kings 9–11—the one that best captures or reflects the dynamics of what these chapters are all about?

_____

_____

19. List any lingering questions you have about 1 Kings 9–11.

_____

_____

_____

For the Group

You may want to focus your discussion for lesson 3 on the following issues, themes, and concepts. (These things will likely reflect what group members have learned in their individual study of this week's passage, although they'll also have made discoveries in other areas as well.)

- The limits, or failed potential, of wisdom
- The uncontrollable dangers of idolatry
- The shallowness of outward security and material prosperity
- God's character as revealed by His words to Solomon and His dealings with him

The following numbered questions in lesson 3 may stimulate your best and most helpful discussion: 1, 7, 9, 14, and 15.

Remember to look also at the "For Thought and Discussion" questions in the margin.

1. Peter J. Leithart, *1 and 2 Kings* (Grand Rapids, MI: Baker, 2006), 82.
2. *New Geneva Study Bible* (Nashville: Thomas Nelson, 1995), introduction to 1 Kings: "Characteristics and Themes."
3. Leithart, 21.
4. *ESV Study Bible* (Wheaton, IL: Crossway, 2008), on 1 Kings 11:34-39.

1 KINGS 12–16

Division and Danger

Israel has been in rebellion against the house of David to this day.

1 KINGS 12:19

1. In chapter 12, how would you evaluate and describe Rehoboam's character and personality?

_____

_____

_____

2. In what ways does Jeroboam at first seem like a hero for Israel?

_____

_____

3. What is the particular significance of the statement made in 12:15 by the author of 1 Kings?

_____

_____

_____

4. In what ways does Rehoboam's leadership display a lack of skill and understanding?

_____

For Thought and Discussion: What important core principles and dynamics for successful leadership are contained in the words the elders gave to King Rehoboam in 12:7?

Optional Application: The wisdom of the elders in 12:7 is contrasted with the cocky foolishness of the younger men in 12:10-11. What lesson might be here for us today? And what connection do you see here with the apostle Peter's words in 1 Peter 5:5?

5. What do the events of chapter 12 reveal about God's sovereignty, His grace, and His justice?

_____

_____

_____

This turn of events (12:15). More literally, this phrase is the word *twist* in Hebrew. God has a way of "twisting" things so that the evil that a person intends toward others will end up hurting himself.

To fulfill the word the Lord had spoken (12:15). The Lord's Word is frequently shown in 1 and 2 Kings as something active, authoritative, and certain of fulfillment. Notice, for example, how many times the phrase "word of the LORD" is used in 1 Kings 13, and in what ways. And notice how the fulfillment of the particular Word of the Lord spoken through the prophet Ahijah is emphasized in 12:15, 14:18, and 15:29.

> "Rehoboam acts willfully, stupidly, brazenly, with foolish bravado, but the division is not ultimately Rehoboam's doing but Yahweh's. . . . Yahweh sovereignly rules even in the midst of human stupidity, ensuring that his promise to Jeroboam comes to pass. Yahweh fulfills his word."[1]

6. In chapter 13, what exactly did the "man of God" do right, and what did he do wrong?

_____

_____

_____

7. What is chapter 13 meant to teach us about God's standards for His prophets? And what relation do those standards have for any of God's people today?

_____

_____

_____

_____

_____

8. What does chapter 13 reveal about the character of Jeroboam, and how would you compare this with what you've seen earlier about him?

_____

_____

_____

9. Through the words of the prophet Ahijah in 14:7-11, what specific punishment does God pronounce against Jeroboam, and for what specific reasons?

_____

_____

_____

10. Compare the prophet Ahijah's words to Jeroboam in 11:31-39 with those spoken here in 14:7-11. What do they together reveal about the Lord's treatment of Jeroboam?

_____

_____

_____

11. What prophecy concerning Israel's future does Ahijah speak about in 14:14-16, and what is its significance?

_____

For Thought and Discussion: We see in 14:13 that Jeroboam's ailing son was the only person among Jeroboam's family in whom the Lord "found anything good," yet this son is not allowed to live. What tensions and questions does this create in our understanding of God's sovereignty, justice, and grace?

_____

_____

12. From what you see in 14:21-31, how would you summarize the spiritual condition of Judah during the reign of Rehoboam?

_____

_____

_____

Detestable practices (14:24). This is translated as _abominations_ in many English versions. "The sins spoken of here are acts of sexual immorality and idolatry, considered not as cultic acts in God's special sanctuary presence, but as acts of covenantal idolatry committed in his land. If they do these things, they will be vomited out of the land."[2]

13. The deaths of both Rehoboam and Jeroboam are reported in chapter 14. From the accounts given of their reigns in 1 Kings, what are the most important facts God wants us to understand about each man?

a. Rehoboam of Judah

_____

_____

b. Jeroboam of Israel

_____

_____

14. The reigns of several more kings (over a span of about half a century) are quickly presented in chapters 15 and 16. From the evidence you see in these chapters, what does God want His people to remember most about each of these rulers?

42

a. Abijah (Abijam) of Judah

_____

_____

b. Asa of Judah

_____

_____

c. Nadab of Israel

_____

_____

d. Baasha of Israel

_____

_____

e. Elah of Israel

_____

_____

f. Zimri of Israel

_____

_____

g. Omri of Israel

_____

_____

h. Ahab of Israel (we'll see more of him later in
   1 Kings)

_____

_____

What was right in the eyes of the LORD (15:11). David had done this (see 15:5), and now Asa is said to have done it also. Seven other rulers of Judah will also accomplish it: Jehoshaphat (see 22:43), Joash (see 2 Kings 12:2), Amaziah (see 14:3), Azariah (see 15:3), Jotham (see 15:34), Hezekiah (see 18:3), and Josiah (see 22:2). For many of them, this praise is qualified by the mention of something wrong that they also did. Meanwhile, on Israel's throne, only King Jehu earned similar praise (see 2 Kings 10:30-31).

15. Notice how the Kings narrative accelerates in chapters 15 and 16. What patterns do you see in this rapidly told history? To what degree are they the same patterns we see throughout human history?

_____

_____

_____

16. How does this quickly unfolding account seem to emphasize the lack of fresh vigor and dynamic development and progress in Israel?

_____

_____

_____

Baasha killed Nadab . . . and succeeded him as king (15:28). Jeroboam's son Nadab was his only descendant to succeed him on Israel's throne. God promised Jeroboam an enduring dynasty (see 11:38) if he fully obeyed Him, a condition Jeroboam quickly violated. The violent transfer of power from Jeroboam's family to Baasha is the first of many such upheavals in the northern kingdom's history. "In portraying the divided kingdom," the author of 1 and

44

2 Kings "points out important differences between the two realms. Kingship in Judah was relatively stable under the descendants of David, but kingship in Israel was unstable, and there was a succession of dynasties."[3] The following chart shows the contrast, with a ruler's reign averaging seventeen years in Judah, but only ten in Israel:

For Further Study:
First Kings 16:34 records the fulfillment of a prophecy made five hundred years earlier by Joshua, after he had conquered the city of Jericho. Read about this prophecy in Joshua 6:26.

	Number of Kings	Number of Dynasties	Duration of Kingdom
JUDAH	20	1	344 years
ISRAEL	20	9	208 years

Omri (16:23). Militarily and politically, this king seems to have attained more prominence than previous rulers of the northern kingdom, but his accomplishments ultimately count for nothing to the author of Scripture. "From the standpoint of a political historian, Omri would be considered one of the more important rulers in the northern kingdom. He established a powerful dynasty and made Samaria the capital city. . . . Yet in spite of Omri's political importance, his reign is dismissed in six verses (16:23-28)."[4]

Baal (16:31-32). This was a Canaanite storm god, thought to have power for bringing rains and making the earth fertile. In Canaanite religion, Baal "is the son of the high god El and husband of the goddess Anat; his enemies are Yam ('Sea') and Mot ('Death'); his weapons are thunder and lightning; and his symbolic representation is the bull. Baal worship presented an attractive alternative or supplement to the worship of the Lord (Yahweh) for many Israelites throughout their time in Canaan, no doubt partly because that land was so utterly dependent on rain for its fertility."[5]

17. What do you think are the most important lessons God wants us to learn from these kings about sin and disobedience?

45

_____

_____

_____

18. What would you select as the key verse or passage in 1 Kings 12–16—the one that best captures or reflects the dynamics of what these chapters are all about?

_____

_____

19. List any lingering questions you have about 1 Kings 12–16.

_____

_____

_____

For the Group

You may want to focus your discussion for lesson 4 on the following issues, themes, and concepts. (These things will likely reflect what group members have learned in their individual study of this week's passage, although they'll also have made discoveries in other areas as well.)

• The causes of divisions among God's people
• The corrupting, pervasive power of idolatry
• The appropriate standards and obligations for those who speak God's words
• The instability that results from rejecting God's ways
• Legitimate versus nonlegitimate worship
• God's faithfulness in continuing to communicate with His people
• The inevitability of consequences for our actions
• Faithfulness to God as the most important factor in shaping our destinies

The following numbered questions in lesson 4 may stimulate your best and most helpful discussion: 12, 15, 16, and 17.

Remember to look also at the "For Thought and Discussion" questions in the margin.

1. Peter J. Leithart, *1 and 2 Kings* (Grand Rapids, MI: Baker, 2006), 95.
2. James B. Jordan, "The Abomination of Desolation, part 4a: Abominable and Detestable," *Biblical Horizons*, 31, http://www.biblicalhorizons.com/bh/bh031.htm, as quoted by Leithart, 108.
3. *New Geneva Study Bible* (Nashville: Thomas Nelson, 1995), introduction to 1 Kings: "Characteristics and Themes."
4. *NIV Study Bible* (Grand Rapids: Zondervan, 1985), introduction to 1 Kings: "Theme: Kingship and Covenant."
5. *ESV Study Bible* (Wheaton, IL: Crossway, 2008), on 1 Kings 16:31-33.

1 KINGS 17–22

Elijah: Voice of Judgment

Is that you, you troubler of Israel?

1 KINGS 18:17

1. In all the things you see happening in chapters 17–22 to King Ahab, how does God most clearly reveal His sovereignty, His grace, and His justice?

_____

_____

_____

2. In what notable ways in these chapters can you see Elijah's clear obedience to the Lord? How is he an example of faithful obedience?

_____

_____

_____

3. What miracles and supernatural actions are highlighted in the story of Elijah's ministry, and what do they together say about God?

_____

_____

_____

For Further Study: Notice how the story of Elijah and the widow of Zarephath in chapter 17 is mentioned by Jesus in Luke 4:23-26, when he speaks in the synagogue at Nazareth. For what point or purpose does Jesus bring up that story on that occasion? Notice also the account in Luke 7:11-16 of Jesus raising to life the dead son of a widow. How is that miracle similar to what Elijah did for the son of the widow in Zarephath?

Optional Application: How does the strength of your own faith line up with the faith principles taught in 1 Kings 17? In what ways can you strengthen your trust in God in light of what you learn here?

Optional Application: Read the description given of Elijah as a man of prayer in James 5:17-18, plus the statements about prayer in 5:16. What does God most want you to learn about prayer from Elijah, a man who is "just like" you (5:17)?

4. What principles for living by faith do you see in chapter 17?

_____

_____

_____

5. How would you describe the power of Elijah's prayer in 17:20-21?

_____

_____

_____

6. The widow of Zarephath calls Elijah a "man of God" (17:18,24). In what ways is Elijah's story similar to that of the "man of God" in chapter 13, and in what ways is it significantly different?

_____

_____

_____

7. How is Elijah shown to be a bringer or channel of dynamic life from God?

_____

_____

_____

8. In chapter 18, how would you summarize what was actually accomplished in the famous encounter on Mount Carmel between Elijah and the prophets of Baal? Why, for God and for His people, was this incident important?

_____

_____

_____

_____

9. From the evidence in 1 Kings 18, what are the most important things Elijah understands about God's personality and character, especially in contrast to that of Baal?

_____

_____

_____

10. How does Elijah show that he is in control of the situation throughout chapter 18?

_____

_____

_____

11. How would you analyze the power of Elijah's prayer in 18:36-37?

_____

_____

_____

The power of the LORD came on Elijah and . . . he ran ahead of Ahab all the way to Jezreel (18:46). "This dramatic scene, with the Lord's prophet running before the king and the Lord himself racing behind him riding his mighty thundercloud chariot, served as a powerful appeal to Ahab to break once for all with Baal and henceforth to rule as the servant of the Lord."[1] "A runner before a king is a herald and a king's servant, and Elijah returns to Jezreel to announce that the blessing of Yahweh has returned to the land and to proclaim the return of the king to one of his chief cities. He is 'before Ahab' in the sense that he is 'before Yahweh' (17:1), a servant to the king. Yet, in another sense, Elijah is 'in front of' the king, leading the way."[2]

12. How consistent is Elijah's action in 19:3 with what you've seen of him earlier? How would you explain what Elijah does here?

Optional
Application: From
what you see in this
chapter, what is God
able to provide to
those who serve and
follow Him? And what
is your own current
need for any of those
things? Express this
need to the Lord in
prayer.

**Optional
Application:** Twice
the Lord asks, "What
are you doing here,
Elijah?" (19:9,13). How
would *you* answer
that question from
the Lord regarding
your own life situ-
ation? What is your
purpose in being
where you are?

**For Thought and
Discussion:** Review
the things that Elijah
witnesses in 19:11-12.
What typical pattern
do they suggest for
how God often deals
with His people?

For Further Study:
Worship the Lord for
His majesty, great-
ness, and holiness
as you observe how
He is associated with
earthquake, wind,
and fire in these pas-
sages: Genesis 19:24;
Exodus 9:23; 2 Samuel
22:11; Psalm 11:6;
18:10; 104:3; Isaiah
29:6; Ezekiel 13:13;
Nahum 1:3.

13. In James 5:17, Elijah is described as "a man
just like us." How do you see that humanity of
Elijah here in chapter 19?

_____

_____

_____

14. In what ways does God most clearly demonstrate His grace to Elijah in chapter 19?

_____

_____

_____

15. What does Elijah most need to learn through
the words God speaks to him in chapter 19?

_____

_____

_____

16. Notice especially God's communication with
Elijah in 19:11-12. What was more important
here—*what* God said to him, or *how* He
said it?

_____

_____

17. How correct is Elijah in his assessment of the
situation in 19:10 and 19:14? Is there any indication that God either agrees or disagrees with
his assessment?

_____

_____

_____

18. What possible significance do you see in the three tasks the Lord assigns to Elijah in 19:15-17? In particular, what might be their effect on Ahab and his reign?

_____

_____

_____

_____

_____

19. In 19:19-21, what is most memorable and significant to you in the way that Elijah called Elisha and in the way Elisha responded?

_____

_____

20. In chapter 20, what were the major developments in the conflict between Ahab of Israel and Ben-Hadad of Syria?

_____

_____

_____

21. Why do you think these details of this particular conflict were included in Scripture? What is their point?

_____

_____

_____

For Further Study: In Romans 11:1-6, how does Paul apply the words exchanged between Elijah and the Lord in 1 Kings 19:14 and 19:18? What does God's answer say about His righteousness, faithfulness, and mercy?

For Thought and Discussion: How does God's guidance of His people today compare with how He guided Elijah in his life?

Optional Application: In 1 Kings 20, Ahab failed to see clearly that Ben-Hadad was an enemy of Israel. Notice in Philippians 3:18-19 that Paul speaks of those who are "enemies of the cross." Who are the enemies of the cross today that we should be aware of, and what should be our response to them?

"The Bible teaches an enmity that goes to the bone. For the Christian there can be no compromise with the enemy, but only battle until victory. . . . Far from deleting enmity from history, Christianity immeasurably and fundamentally deepens it."[3]

A man I had determined should die (20:42). An
NIV footnote reads, "The Hebrew term refers
to the irrevocable giving over of things or
persons to the Lord, often by totally destroy-
ing them." Other translations of this phrase in
20:42 include "the man whom I had devoted to
destruction" (ESV, NASB) or "appointed to utter
destruction" (NKJV). See God's explanation in
Deuteronomy 20:16-18.

22. What does chapter 21 reveal about the heart
and mind of both Ahab and his wife Jezebel?

_____

_____

_____

"Ahab and Jezebel . . . miss the most
important factor in the situation: there is
a God from whom no secrets are hid, a
God before whom all the thoughts and
intentions of the heart are open and
revealed."[4]

23. In what ways did Ahab "sell" himself "to do evil
in the eyes of the Lord"? (21:20)?

_____

_____

_____

24. What specific events in the future does God
prophesy to Ahab through Elijah in 21:17-24?

_____

_____

_____

_____

25. In 21:25-26, notice the further condemnation of Ahab given by the author of 1 Kings. What explanation would you give for the surprising mercy God showed to Ahab in 21:27-29?

_____

_____

_____

26. Allegorically, how is Naboth's story in 1 Kings 21 like the story of Jesus?

_____

_____

_____

Ahab. This man's name means "the LORD judges." In 1 Kings 21, the Lord God brings final earthly judgment upon him.

---

27. How would you describe the power of the story (in chapter 22) of the prophet Micaiah and his encounter with the two kings? What is it that makes this passage so gripping?

_____

_____

_____

Is there not a prophet of the LORD here (22:7). "True prophets preached only what God told them to proclaim. Their messages focused on covenant issues, particularly how the practice of idolatry would result in punishment and, ultimately, expulsion from the land. . . . Their declarations also emphasized future events. In fact, their predictions and their subsequent fulfillments help structure the story. . . . God makes sure that the words the true prophets declare come true because they are in fact his word."[5]

For Further Study: In 21:26, we read that Ahab "behaved in the vilest manner by going after idols." Yet again we see *idolatry* as a recurring theme in 1 and 2 Kings. How do Paul's words in Romans 1:18-32 relate to idolatry, and what are the most important points he makes?

For Thought and Discussion: As you think about the conflicting messages given in chapter 22 by God's prophet Micaiah and by the false prophets, what conflict, if any, between true and false prophets do you see taking place today?

For Thought and Discussion: Does God "set a trap" for Ahab in this chapter? How would you analyze His treatment here of this king? And what does that tell us about His character and what we today should expect from God?

28. From the evidence recorded in chapter 22, what does God want His people to remember most about each of these rulers?

a. Jehoshaphat of Judah

_____

_____

b. Ahaziah of Israel (we'll see more of him in 2 Kings 1)

_____

_____

29. What would you select as the key verse or passage in 1 Kings 17–22, the one that best captures or reflects the dynamics of what these chapters are all about?

_____

_____

_____

30. Recall the guidelines given for our thought-life in Philippians 4:8: "Whatever is true, whatever is noble, whatever is right, whatever is pure, whatever is lovely, whatever is admirable—if anything is excellent or praiseworthy—*think about such things*" (emphasis added). As you reflect on all you've read in 1 Kings, what stands out to you as being particularly *true*, or *noble*, or *right*, or *pure*, or *lovely*, or *admirable*, or *excellent*, or *praiseworthy*—and therefore well worth thinking more about?

_____

_____

_____

31. What has been the strongest example to you in the book of 1 Kings of someone doing what was right and good in the eyes of the Lord? What has been the strongest example here of someone doing what was wrong in His eyes?

_____

_____

_____

32. List any lingering questions you have about
    1 Kings 17–22.

_____

_____

_____

For the Group

You may want to focus your discussion for lesson
5 on the following issues, themes, and concepts.
(These things will likely reflect what group members have learned in their individual study of this
week's passage, although they'll also have made
discoveries in other areas as well.)

- God's gracious provision for His servants
- God's supreme power over the forces of evil
- The reassurance that believers often need from
  God
- God's committed opposition to evil
- The corrupt ruthlessness in the hearts of those
  who oppose God
- Our need to clearly oppose evil
- The tragic destiny of the wicked
- Our need to rely fully on God for all things
- The ongoing corruption of idolatry
- The intense battle between true and false
  prophecy, and the final assured victory of the
  truth
- The rarity of godly leadership

    The following numbered questions in lesson 5
may stimulate your best and most helpful discussion: 1, 2, 4, 9, 14, 25, and 26.
    Remember to look also at the "For Thought and
Discussion" questions in the margin.

1. *NIV Study Bible* (Grand Rapids, MI: Zondervan, 1985), on
   1 Kings 18:46.
2. Peter J. Leithart, *1 and 2 Kings* (Grand Rapids, MI: Baker,
   2006), 137.

3. Leithart, 151.
4. Leithart, 156.
5. Paul R. House, *1, 2 Kings*, vol. 8 in NEW AMERICAN COMMENTARY, ed. E. Ray Clendenen (Nashville: Broadman, Holman, 1995), 79.

2 KINGS 1–7

Elisha: Hand of Power

Don't be afraid.... Those who are with us are more than those who are with them.

2 KINGS 6:16

(Notice that the story of King Ahab, as well as the stories of the prophets Elijah and Elisha, overlap the book division between 1 and 2 Kings. The break between the books is mostly an artificial one.)

1. Proverbs 2:1-5 tells about the sincere person who truly longs for wisdom and understanding and who searches the Scriptures for it as if there were treasure buried there. Such a person, this passage says, will come to understand the fear of the Lord and discover the knowledge of God. As you continue exploring these two books of Kings, what "hidden treasure" would you like God to help you find here—to show you what God and His wisdom are really like? If you have this desire, how would you express it in your own words of prayer to God?

_____

_____

_____

_____

_____

Optional Application: As 2 Kings opens, Israel's King Ahaziah consults with a false god in his time of need instead of looking to the Lord, and for this he is judged by God (see 2 Kings 1:1-4,15-17). Who or what are *you* most likely to turn to as a substitute for God?

Optional Application: In what specific ways do you sense God's approval at this time in your life? Express to Him your gratitude for this.

Baal-Zebub (1:2). This name means "Lord of the flies" and is thought to be an intentional corruption of "Baal-Zebul," meaning "Baal is prince" or "Baal is mighty." This name occurs only here in the Old Testament. In the New Testament it appears with the alternate spelling "Beelzebub" as another name for Satan, "the prince of demons" (see Matthew 10:25; 12:24-27; Mark 3:22; Luke 11:15-19).

2. How does the prophet Elijah continue to demonstrate God's power in 2 Kings 1?

_____

_____

_____

_____

3. The stories of Elijah and Elisha represent the heart and core of the combined books of Kings. What significant character aspects and traits are revealed in 2 Kings 2 about each of these servants of God?

a. Elijah

_____

_____

b. Elisha

_____

_____

4. In what specific ways does God show His approval of the ministries of both Elijah and Elisha in these chapters?

_____

_____

_____

60

"The renewal movement ultimately fails, for Israel goes to exile despite the ministries of Elijah and Elisha. Here is another dimension of the evangelical thrust of 1–2 Kings: wisdom cannot save Israel; the temple cannot save Israel; kings cannot save Israel. Prophets provide life for those who hear and believe their words, but ultimately not even the prophetic movement prevents Israel's destruction."[1]

5. How would you describe the relationship Elijah and Elisha have with each other, from the evidence we see in these chapters?

_____

_____

_____

6. How would you compare and contrast Elisha's request (in response to Elijah) in 2 Kings 2:9-10 with Solomon's request (in response to the Lord) in 1 Kings 3:5-14?

_____

_____

_____

7. How does Elisha most clearly demonstrate in these chapters that he, like Elijah, is truly a prophet of the living God?

_____

_____

_____

8. a. How many purposes can you identify behind the miracles that Elisha performs in these chapters?

_____

Optional Application: How does the breadth and boldness of Elisha's request in 2 Kings 2:9 compare with what *you* are asking God for? With encouragement from Elisha's example with Elijah, what *more* can you now boldly request from God, in accordance with His will?

For Further Study: Compare Elijah's departure from the earth (as described in 2:1 and 2:11) with what happened to Enoch in Genesis 5:24. (For more on Enoch's departure, see Hebrews 11:5.)

For Further Study:
We read in 4:14 that the Shunammite woman "has no son and her husband is old." Observe how Scripture highlights God's grace to childless women in Genesis 11:30; 17:16-19; 25:21-26; 29:31; 30:22-24; Judges 13:2-5,24; Psalm 113:9; Isaiah 54:1; Luke 1:5-25. Together what do these indicate about God's character?

Optional Application: What actions or attitudes of faith that you see in the Shunammite woman in 2 Kings 4 can you apply in your life, especially in regard to any stress or serious needs you face?

For Further Study: God used both Elijah (see 1 Kings 17:17-23) and Elisha (see 2 Kings 4:18-36) to restore life to boys who had died. Compare these miracles to similar ones in 2 Kings 13:20-21; Luke 7:14-15; 8:52-56; John 11:38-44; Acts 9:40-41; 20:9-20. Together what do these miracles tell us about God?

_____

_____

b. Which of Elisha's miracles are most impressive to you, and why?

_____

_____

9. What do you think is our full and proper response today to the miracles God did through the ministries of both Elijah and Elisha?

_____

_____

_____

10. What are the most significant truths that both Elijah and Elisha seem to understand deeply about God?

_____

_____

11. From the evidence you see early in 2 Kings 3, what does God want His people to remember most about King Joram of Israel?

_____

_____

12. How does God most clearly show His power and sovereignty in Israel's battle with Moab in chapter 3?

_____

_____

13. In 4:8-37, how does the Shunammite woman demonstrate her faith?

_____

_____

14. a. What would you say is Naaman's root problem as evidenced in chapter 5?

    _____

    _____

    b. What would you say is Gehazi's root problem in the same chapter?

    _____

    _____

    c. How does God demonstrate His sovereignty, grace, and justice in the ways He deals here with both Naaman and Gehazi?

    _____

    _____

    _____

Optional Application: What tendencies do you see in your own life that match the particular character flaws of either Naaman or Gehazi (or both) in 2 Kings 5? If you see those tendencies in yourself, what has God already done for you about them, and what can you expect Him (and ask Him in faith) to do about them in the future?

Optional Application: In the way that Naaman was brought to faith, what personal encouragement do you see for your evangelism and your witness for Christ?

"Certainly evangelism can take many forms. For instance, the slave girl simply tells Naaman where he can get help, yet she begins his healing and conversion journey (2 Kings 5:1-3). On the other hand, Elisha tells Naaman how to be healed, which forces the Syrian to trust God, which in turn leads to a personal discovery of Yahweh. Both the prophet and the girl share a word appropriate in that situation ... and this obedience ... is the heart of evangelism. Specific methods are useful when this central obedience exists but only then."[2]

15. a. How does Naaman express his new faith in the one true God? And how firm does that faith appear to be?

    _____

b. What evangelism principles do you see represented in how Naaman came to faith in God?

_____

_____

_____

16. How is Elisha's ministry like the ministry of Jesus in His time on earth?

_____

_____

_____

The company of the prophets (6:1). This term (also translated sometimes as "the sons of the prophets") is found often in 1 and 2 Kings (see, for example, 1 Kings 20:35; 2 Kings 2:3,15; 4:1,38; 9:1). "The value of communities of faith emerges repeatedly . . . and remains vital today. The 'sons of the prophets' ate together, worked together, and witnessed together. They shared a common calling, a common goal, and a common suffering. Their victories were also shared. Clearly, the primary elements of a confessional community transcend time and space. Churches can recapture their power only when they are unified under God's plan for Christ's body."[3]

Iron axhead (6:5). In Israel at this time, such a tool would be both rare and costly, and extremely difficult to replace.

We cooked my son and ate him (6:29). God's people were long ago warned about such cannibalism as a curse for their disobedience. (See Leviticus 26:27-29 and Deuteronomy 28:52-57; also Lamentations 2:20; 4:10; and Ezekiel 5:10.)

17. How does the long account of Ben-Hadad's siege of Samaria (see 6:24–7:20) demonstrate the ways in which severe trials bring out our true character?

_____

_____

_____

18. What would you select as the key verse or passage in 2 Kings 1–7—the one that best captures or reflects the dynamics of what these chapters are all about?

_____

_____

19. List any lingering questions you have about 2 Kings 1–7.

_____

_____

_____

_____

For the Group

You may want to focus your discussion for lesson 6 on the following issues, themes, and concepts. (These things will likely reflect what group members have learned in their individual study of this week's passage, although they'll also have made discoveries in other areas as well.)

- God's nature as revealed in His sovereignty over the events in our lives
- Faith and obedience
- Evangelism
- Unity and community among God's people
- The surpassing, healing, life-giving power available to God's servants
- The reality on earth of the unseen forces of God's heavenly armies
- The certainty that God's words will be fulfilled

The following numbered questions in lesson 6 may stimulate your best and most helpful discussion: 3, 10, 13, 14, and 17.

Remember to look also at the "For Thought and Discussion" questions in the margin.

1. Peter J. Leithart, *1 and 2 Kings* (Grand Rapids, MI: Baker, 2006), 127.
2. Paul R. House, *1, 2 Kings*, vol. 8 in NEW AMERICAN COMMENTARY, ed. E. Ray Clendenen (Nashville: Broadman, Holman, 1995), 315.
3. House, 316.

2 KINGS 8–17

Disintegration

The LORD had seen how bitterly everyone in Israel, whether slave or free, was suffering.

2 KINGS 14:26

1. How does the incident in 2 Kings 8:1-6 show God's care for those who are destitute or defenseless?

_____

_____

_____

For Thought and Discussion: Expanding on the imagery expressed in 8:19, how is Jesus serving now as "a lamp for David and his descendants forever"? And how is His church also fulfilling that role?

He married a daughter of Ahab (8:18). Judah's King Jehoram, who would promote in his kingdom the same idolatry that had corrupted the northern kingdom, married Athaliah, the daughter of Israel's King Ahab. "The ruling dynasties of north and south were now linked by ideology and by blood."[1] Athaliah will later play a notorious role in Judah's history.

2. What promise from God are we reminded of in 2 Kings 8:19? (Look back at the promise spoken earlier in 1 Kings 11:36.) Why do you think the book's author brings this up again at this particular point in the narrative?

_____

_____

_____

3. From the evidence recorded in chapter 8, what does God want His people to remember most about each of the following rulers?

   a. Jehoram of Judah

   _____

   _____

   b. Ahaziah of Judah

   _____

   _____

4. For helpful background on the events of chapter 9, refer back to the words of instruction and prophecy given by the Lord to Elijah in 1 Kings 19:16-17. How are these words now being played out?

   _____

   _____

   _____

5. In chapters 9–10, how would you analyze Jehu's leadership skills and effectiveness?

   _____

   _____

   _____

6. How do Jehu's actions in chapters 9–10 affect both Israel and Judah?

   _____

   _____

   _____

   _____

"Few events in the history of the divided kingdom are as momentous as Jehu's purge of the political and religious leaders of Israel and Judah."[2]

Optional Application: King Jehu was able to say to Jehonadab, "Come with me and see my zeal for the LORD" (10:16). Will *you* be able to say something like this to people you encounter? What "zeal for the LORD" is visible and apparent in your life?

7. From the evidence in chapters 9–10, what does God want His people to remember most about Jehu of Israel?

_____

_____

This is the word of the LORD that he spoke through his servant Elijah (9:36). Elijah prophesied this judgment on Jezebel in 1 Kings 21:23.

Jehonadab (10:15). This man expressed agreement with Jehu's campaign to root out Ahab's legacy in Israel. More than two centuries later, the prophet Jeremiah would commend the descendants of Jehonadab for still remaining faithful to his legacy of ascetic devotion to the Lord. The account is given in Jeremiah 35 (where his name is spelled "Jonadab"). Through Jeremiah, the Lord promised that Jehonadab "will never fail to have a man to serve me" (Jeremiah 35:19).

---

8. Notice the specific praise given by the Lord to Jehu in 10:30 and the qualification added by the author of 2 Kings in 10:31. Looking back over the record of Jehu's reign, what do you think the Lord had most in mind when He said what He did to Jehu in verse 30? And what did the author of 2 Kings have most in mind when he added what he did in verse 31?

_____

_____

_____

For Further Study:
Notice the covenants
Jehoiada initiates
between the Lord
and His people
and their king, and
between the king and
the people (see 11:17).

For Further Study:
See the covenant
ceremony led by
Moses in Exodus
24:3-8 (as the model
for Jehoiada's actions
in 2 Kings 11:17). See
also the covenant
renewal ceremony
led by Joshua in
Joshua 24:1-27.

**Optional
Application:** The
people covenanted
"that they would be
the LORD's people"
(11:17). How can God's
people today best
express that same
commitment in an
appropriate way that
pleases God?

*Athaliah . . . proceeded to destroy the whole
royal family* (11:1). Athaliah was the daughter of Ahab whom Judah's King Jehoram had
married, uniting the dynasties of north and
south (see 8:18,26). She was the only woman,
and the only usurper, ever to rule from David's
throne. She displayed contempt for all that his
throne meant by acting to murder his remaining descendants in the royal line. "This attempt
to completely destroy the house of David was
an attack on God's redemptive plan—a plan
that centered in the Messiah, which the Davidic
covenant promised."[3]

9. How do the events in chapter 11 demonstrate
   God's sovereignty?

   _____

   _____

10. Summarize the actions taken by Jehoiada the
    priest in chapters 11 and in 12:1-9. How does
    this man demonstrate strong and worthy
    leadership?

    _____

    _____

    _____

A copy of the covenant (11:12). Many Bible
scholars believe this "covenant" to be God's
rules for kings laid out in Deuteronomy
17:14-20.

*Jehoiada then made a covenant between the
LORD and the king and people that they
would be the LORD's people. He also made
a covenant between the king and the
people* (11:17). "Literally the text says . . . 'the

covenant' . . . which indicates that a previous covenantal model was followed. The covenant that is made between God and the people is a reminder and renewal of the pledges made in Exodus 24:8."[4] (See Exodus 24:3-8.)

---

11. What is significant about the actions taken by the people of Judah in 11:18? How would you compare and contrast their actions with what King Jehu had earlier done in Israel in 10:18-28?

_____

_____

_____

_____

Optional Application: After the renewal of the Mosaic covenant (see 11:17), the people tore down the temple of Baal and smashed altars and idols. Is there any "idol-smashing" that needs to take place in your life at this time?

"Since God is unique and since idols are condemned throughout Scripture, contemporary believers need to make a fearless inventory of idols in their lives."[5]

"Idols are lifeless and therefore cannot impart life. Lifeless idols only make for lifeless people. When the initial titillation has passed, idolatry quickly yields to dryness and death. The signs of this spiritual exhaustion are everywhere in twenty-first-century culture, which has become a culture of 'whatever'—not only the whatever of 'anything goes,' but the whatever of 'and who cares anyway?' This is the end result of a culture that has been built on idols of success, money, pleasure, self-indulgence, sex."[6]

12. How does the reign of Joash (Jehoash) of Judah slide downward into disappointment and tragedy? And what do you think was the cause of this?

_____

_____

_____

13. From the evidence in chapter 12, what does God want His people to remember most about Joash (Jehoash) of Judah?

_____

_____

14. The description of Jehoahaz in 13:1-9 is one of the fullest examples of the general formula followed by the author of 1 and 2 Kings to describe the reign of each ruler. From this full example, what elements in this formula can you identify, and what is the importance of each one?

_____

_____

_____

15. In 13:14-19, what is the chief significance in the things that were said and done during King Joash's meeting with the dying prophet Elisha?

_____

_____

16. From the evidence in chapter 13, what does God want His people to remember most about these rulers?

a. Jehoahaz of Israel

_____

_____

b. Jehoash of Israel

_____

_____

17. Look carefully at 13:22-23. What is most sig-
    nificant about this summary statement of the
    Lord's heart and perspective toward rebellious
    Israel (the northern kingdom)?

    _____

    _____

    _____

18. From the evidence recorded in chapter 14, what
    does God want His people to remember most
    about each of the following rulers?

    a. Amaziah of Judah

    _____

    _____

    b. Jeroboam II of Israel

    _____

    _____

19. What does 2 Kings 14:26-27 reveal about God's
    character, especially in light of Israel's persis-
    tent spiritual corruption?

    _____

    _____

    _____

20. From the evidence in chapter 15, what does God
    want His people to remember most about these
    rulers?

    a. Azariah of Judah

    _____

    _____

b. Zechariah of Israel

_____

_____

c. Shallum of Israel

_____

_____

d. Menahem of Israel

_____

_____

e. Pekahiah of Israel

_____

_____

f. Pekah of Israel

_____

_____

g. Jotham of Judah

_____

_____

21. In chapter 16, what things do you see King Ahaz doing wrong?

_____

_____

_____

22. From the evidence in chapter 16, what does God want His people to remember most about Ahaz of Judah?

_____

_____

_____

23. From the evidence in chapter 17, what does God want His people to remember most about Hoshea, the last king of Israel?

_____

_____

_____

24. Summarize the particular military and political developments involved in the fall of Israel, as you see them playing out in chapter 17.

_____

_____

_____

25. Reflect carefully on the reasons stated in 17:7-23 for Israel's final fall into captivity.

a. What were the specific actions or attitudes on Israel's part that brought about this judgment from God?

_____

_____

b. What clear indications are given of the seriousness of Israel's sins?

_____

_____

c. How did the southern kingdom of Judah share in the sins of the northern kingdom of Israel?

_____

_____

d. How is God's love for His people demonstrated in these words?

_____

_____

For Thought and Discussion: In the tragic summary given in 2 Kings 17 of the reasons for Israel's fall, what lessons are there for His people today? In what way do these words reflect God's expectations of us?

For Further Study: "They worshiped *idols*, though the LORD had said, 'You shall not do this'" (2 Kings 17:12, emphasis added). Review what the following New Testament passages teach us about the continuing serious danger of idolatry: 1 Corinthians 10:1-14; Galatians 5:19-21; Colossians 3:5-6; 1 John 5:21.

Optional Application: What do you understand to be your own most serious temptations to idolatry? How does God want you to respond to this danger? (Review the New Testament passages on idolatry listed in the "For Further Study" note.)

75

For Further Study: Observe what three major eighth-century prophets—Hosea, Amos, and Isaiah—proclaim about idolatry in these passages: Isaiah 2:6-9; 44:9-20; Hosea 2:2-13; Amos 2:4-5. How do these prophetic words reinforce the message against idolatry in 1 and 2 Kings?

For Thought and Discussion: What do you see as the most prevalent forms of idolatry in our culture today? Which forms of idolatry seem to be the most dangerous temptations for the church?

The Israelites had sinned against the LORD their God. . . . They worshiped other gods (17:7). "If Old Testament theology could be summarized in one sentence, it probably would read, 'There is no god but the Lord.' . . . Israel is told to worship only the Lord (Exodus 20:3) and is warned not to bow down to any idol (20:4-5). . . . The author of 1, 2 Kings drives home the anti-idolatry, promonotheism theme repeatedly. . . . A refusal to turn from idolatry ultimately leads to the destruction of both Israel and Judah."[7]

26. What explanation can you give for why God's people were so attracted to idolatry despite being so severely warned about it?

_____

_____

_____

27. In 17:24-41, how does God continue to show His sovereignty and grace toward the people who settled in the land that was once the northern kingdom of Israel (after the Assyrians took captive Israel's people)?

_____

_____

_____

28. What would you select as the key verse or passage in 2 Kings 8–17—the one that best captures or reflects the dynamics of what these chapters are all about?

_____

_____

29. List any lingering questions you have about 2 Kings 8–17.

_____

_____

_____

For the Group

You may want to focus your discussion for lesson 7 on the following issues, themes, and concepts. (These things will likely reflect what group members have learned in their individual study of this week's passage, although they'll also have made discoveries in other areas as well.)

- The damage caused by ruthless, overbearing leadership
- The benefit derived from strong, morally driven, well-balanced leadership
- Our frequent need for revival and reform
- Our continual need to seek the Lord's grace and favor

The following numbered questions in lesson 7 may stimulate your best and most helpful discussion: 9, 10, 25, 26, and 27.

And again, remember to look at the "For Thought and Discussion" questions in the margin.

1. *New Geneva Study Bible* (Nashville: Thomas Nelson, 1995), on 2 Kings 8:18.
2. Paul R. House, *1, 2 Kings*, vol. 8 in NEW AMERICAN COMMENTARY, ed. E. Ray Clendenen (Nashville: Broadman, Holman, 1995), 287.
3. *NIV Study Bible* (Grand Rapids, MI: Zondervan, 1985), on 2 Kings 11:1.
4. House, 299.
5. House, 248.
6. Peter J. Leithart, *1 and 2 Kings* (Grand Rapids, MI: Baker, 2006), 113–114.
7. House, 74.

2 KINGS 18–25

A Final Fall

*My anger will burn against this place and will
not be quenched.*
                                                2 KINGS 22:17

We now reach the final portion of the book of
Kings, dealing with Judah as the only surviving
part of the strong and prosperous kingdom that
once was ruled by David and Solomon.

1. Notice what we're reminded of again in 18:9-12.
   What is it that God wants His people to remember most about Israel's fate? And why do you
   think this is emphasized again here as the story
   of Hezekiah unfolds?

   _____

   _____

   _____

**They had not obeyed the LORD their God, but
had violated his covenant—all that Moses
the servant of the LORD commanded** (18:12).
"Israel's breach of covenant is evident in the
ten violations listed in 17:15-17, numerically
matching the Ten Words [Ten Command-
ments] that summarize the original covenant
in which Israel receives the land"; in 1 and 2
Kings, the author is "justifying God's ways with
Israel by showing that Israel and Judah both

79

Optional Application: How would you compare Hezekiah's personal understanding of God with your own?

sinned in the face of Yahweh's persistent mercy and repeated warnings."[1]

2. a. As chapter 18 closes, how would you summarize the crisis faced by Judah and King Hezekiah?

_____

_____

_____

b. What is needed most from Hezekiah at this time?

_____

_____

3. a. What is Hezekiah's hope, as expressed in 19:1-4?

_____

_____

b. How is that hope further expressed in his prayer in 19:14-19?

_____

_____

c. What are the most important things Hezekiah understands about God's personality and character?

_____

_____

4. What is most significant, and why, in the lengthy prophetic response to Hezekiah's prayer given in 19:20-34? What specific *facts*—past, present, and future—does God want Hezekiah to understand?

_____

_____

_____

_____

5. How would you describe the role that Isaiah plays in Hezekiah's healing, and its significance (see 20:1-11)?

_____

_____

_____

Optional Application: Which of the things said about Hezekiah in 18:5-7 can also be said about you? And which others do you *want* to be true about you? Express your thoughts about this in prayer to God.

Biblical Prophets Who Ministered During the Time of 1 and 2 Kings

Several prophets whose books we read in the Old Testament were active in ministry in Israel and Judah during the years described in 1 and 2 Kings. (Two of them—Isaiah and Jonah—are mentioned in the text of 2 Kings.)

Here's the approximate time periods for the work of these prophets:

• *Jonah, Amos,* and *Hosea* were active in Israel during the reign of Jeroboam II, with Hosea's ministry likely extending through the short reigns of several of the final kings of Israel.

• *Isaiah* and *Micah* were active in Judah during the reigns of Azariah (Uzziah), Jotham, Ahaz, and Hezekiah.

• *Nahum* was active in Judah in the reigns of Manasseh, Amon, and Josiah. *Zephaniah* and *Habakkuk* also worked during the reign of Josiah.

• *Jeremiah* began his ministry in Judah during Josiah's reign, and his work continued through all the final four kings of Judah.

• *Daniel* and *Ezekiel* were among the earliest groups of captives taken to Babylon in the years just before Judah's final fall. Their ministry service was in Babylon.

---

6. From the evidence recorded in chapters 18–20, what does God want His people to remember most about King Hezekiah of Judah?

_____

_____

81

For Thought and Discussion: What appropriate warnings can the people of God receive today through the account of God's response to the actions of King Manasseh?

For Thought and Discussion: In what ways do Josiah's reforms reflect any changes that might be needed in our church today?

7. From the evidence you see in chapter 21, what does God want His people to remember most about each of these rulers?

a. Manasseh of Judah

_____

_____

b. Amon of Judah

_____

_____

8. What is it about Manasseh's actions that were so particularly offensive to God?

_____

_____

9. What prompted the reforms that King Josiah initiated?

_____

_____

"It is difficult, if not impossible, to express adequately the magnitude of Josiah's achievements or those of others whose work was enhanced by his presence. . . . The years of Josiah's rule (ca. 640–609) are a glittering bright spot in the nation's tragic slide to destruction. As such they encourage readers concerning what is possible when obedience overrules rebellion."[2]

10. In regard to the spiritual revival described in 2 Kings 23, how would you summarize its reasons and the results?

_____

_____

_____

"Josiah's iconoclast reformation extends to Bethel and 'all the cities of Samaria (2 Kings 23:15-20), and 1–2 Kings strongly suggests that Josiah's Passover is an all-Israel celebration (2 Kings 23:21-23; cf. 2 Chronicles 35:16-19). Like everything else that Josiah attempts, his bid at reuniting Israel under a Davidic king is futile. Josiah reunites the kingdom just in time for Babylonian exile, and when Nebuchadnezzar besieges Jerusalem, he attacks the capital of an Israel that has lately been liturgically if not politically reunited. Neither Josiah's Torah observance nor his ecumenical efforts save Israel from exile."[3]

11. From the evidence in chapters 22–23, what does God want His people to remember most about King Josiah of Judah?

_____

_____

12. Look back at the prophecy about Josiah given in 1 Kings 13:1-3, almost three centuries before Josiah came to the throne. How exactly did Josiah fulfill this prophecy?

_____

_____

_____

13. Look carefully at the tragic statements in 2 Kings 23:26-27. Why do you think at this particular time the Lord finally decided to bring

83

about Judah's destruction? Why were Josiah's repentance and reforms not enough to avert or extensively delay the national disaster God had ordained?

_____

_____

_____

_____

_____

14. From the evidence in chapter 23, what does God want His people to remember most about King Jehoahaz of Judah?

_____

_____

15. From the evidence you see in chapters 23–24, what does God want His people to remember most about each of these rulers?

a. Jehoiakim of Judah

_____

_____

b. Jehoiachin of Judah

_____

_____

c. Zedekiah of Judah

_____

_____

16. Summarize the particular military and political developments involved in the final fall of Judah, as you see them playing out in the final few chapters of 2 Kings.

_____

_____

17. Look at the summary statements about Judah given in 24:3-4 and 24:20. Why do you think these are so much briefer than the similar statements given in 2 Kings 17 about Israel's final fall, about 140 years earlier?

_____

_____

_____

18. Look back to Solomon's temple dedication prayer in 1 Kings 8:33-52 and notice the various calamities that Solomon mentions as future possibilities. We have seen most of these hardships become realities throughout the rest of 1 and 2 Kings. How well did Israel and Judah's kings and people respond in the way that Solomon envisioned?

_____

_____

_____

_____

_____

19. Review carefully the closing words in 25:27-30. In what ways is this a particularly appropriate ending for these two books of Kings?

_____

_____

_____

20. What would you select as the key verse or passage in 2 Kings 18–25—the one that best captures or reflects the dynamics of what these chapters are all about?

_____

_____

"Thus the final curtain falls on the drama of the divided monarchy. What had been a note of dark despair is illuminated by the light of God's gracious concern for his own. Although God's people had been judged as they must, yet God would be with them even in the midst of their sentence. Jehoiachin's release and renewed enjoyment of life thus stands as a harbinger of the further release and return of all the nation, in accordance with God's promises (cf. Jeremiah 31:18; Lamentations 5:21). The spiritually minded believers perhaps would see in this incident an assurance of God's greater redemption from bondage of those who looked forward to him who gives release and eternal refreshment to all who love his appearing."[4]

"The book of Kings leaves Israel east of Eden, awaiting a return that is not yet come. And so it leaves us, a divided Christendom exiled in modern secularism, enduring the times of the Gentiles. It leaves us in exile, but it does not leave us without hope of return."[5]

21. What has been the strongest example to you throughout the book of 2 Kings of someone doing what was right and good in the eyes of the Lord? What has been the strongest example in this book of someone doing what was wrong in His eyes?

_____

_____

_____

22. List any lingering questions you have about 2 Kings 18–25.

_____

_____

_____

Reviewing 1 and 2 Kings

23. In your understanding, what events in 1 and 2 Kings point most clearly to God's absolute sovereignty?

_____

_____

_____

"First and Second Kings . . . stress God's sovereignty over Israel and all other nations. They claim that God created the earth and therefore has every right to rule the earth. This rule unfolds in accordance with the Lord's character, which means that mercy, justice, righteousness, and salvation work together when God fashions world events. . . . God's absolute rule of all creation undergirds every theological emphasis in 1, 2 Kings."[6]

24. In your understanding, what are the strongest ways in which 1 and 2 Kings point us to mankind's need for Jesus and what He accomplished in His death and resurrection?

For Further Study:
Reflect on the specific words of David in Psalm 18:25-27 about the sovereign ways of God. How do you see these truths played out in 1 and 2 Kings?

87

_____

_____

25. Recall the guidelines given for our thought-life in Philippians 4:8: "Whatever is true, whatever is noble, whatever is right, whatever is pure, whatever is lovely, whatever is admirable—if anything is excellent or praiseworthy—*think about such things*" (emphasis added). As you reflect on all you've read in 1 Kings, what stands out to you as being particularly *true*, or *noble*, or *right*, or *pure*, or *lovely*, or *admirable*, or *excellent*, or *praiseworthy*—and therefore well worth thinking more about?

_____

_____

_____

26. In Isaiah 55:10-11, God reminds us that in the same way that He sends rain and snow from the sky to water the earth and nurture life, so also He sends His words to accomplish specific purposes. What would you suggest are God's primary purposes for the message of 1 and 2 Kings in the lives of His people today?

_____

_____

_____

27. In Romans 15:4, Paul reminds us that the Old Testament Scriptures can give us patience and perseverance on one hand as well as comfort and encouragement on the other. In your own life, how do you see the books of 1 and 2 Kings living up to Paul's description? In what ways do they help meet your personal needs for both perseverance and encouragement?

_____

_____

_____

_____

For the Group

You may want to focus your discussion for lesson 8 on the following issues, themes, and concepts. (These things will likely reflect what group members have learned in their individual study of this week's passage, although they'll also have made discoveries in other areas as well.)

- How God is able to do "immeasurably more than all we ask or imagine, according to his power that is at work within us" (Ephesians 3:20)
- The great worth and blessing of obedience
- The depths of the human sin nature, even in a spiritually "healthy" environment
- The certainty that God will be faithful to keep His promises and follow through with His warnings
- The unchanging fact that God answers prayer
- The fact that there will always be a remnant of faithful believers, even in the midst of rampant rebellion and apostasy
- The far-reaching consequences of sin
- How a strong and growing faith will continue to be tested in progressively more challenging ways
- God's perspective as the only trustworthy and accurate view of history

The following numbered questions in lesson 8 may stimulate your best and most helpful discussion: 2, 3, 4, and 13.

Allow enough discussion time to look back together and review all of 1 and 2 Kings as a whole. You can use the numbered questions 24, 25, 26, and 27 in this lesson to help you do that.

Once more, look also at the questions in the margin under the heading "For Thought and Discussion" in the margin.

1. Peter J. Leithart, *1 and 2 Kings* (Grand Rapids, MI: Baker, 2006), 251.
2. Paul R. House, *1, 2 Kings*, vol. 8 in NEW AMERICAN COMMENTARY, ed. E. Ray Clendenen (Nashville: Broadman, Holman, 1995), 380–381.
3. Leithart, 27.

4. Richard D. Patterson and Hermann J. Austel, *1, 2 Kings,* vol. 4 in THE EXPOSITOR'S BIBLE COMMENTARY, ed. Frank E. Gaebelein (Grand Rapids, MI: Zondervan, 1988), 300.
5. Leithart, 279.
6. House, 28, 81.

STUDY AIDS

For further information on the material in this study, consider the following sources. They can be purchased at such websites as www.christianbook.com and www.amazon.com or your local Christian bookstore should be able to order any of them if it does not carry them. Most seminary libraries have them, as well as many university and public libraries. If a source is out of print, you might be able to find it online.

Commentaries on 1 and 2 Kings

Paul R. House, *1, 2 Kings*, vol. 8 in NEW AMERICAN COMMENTARY, ed. E. Ray Clendenen (Broadman, Holman, 1995).

Peter J. Leithart, *1 and 2 Kings* (Baker, 2006).

Richard D. Patterson and Hermann J. Austel, *1, 2 Kings*, vol. 4 in THE EXPOSITOR'S BIBLE COMMENTARY, ed. Frank E. Gaebelein (Zondervan, 1988).

Iain W. Provan, *1 and 2 Kings*, vol. 7 in NEW INTERNATIONAL BIBLICAL COMMENTARY (Baker, 1993).

Donald J. Wiseman. *1 and 2 Kings: An Introduction and Commentary*, vol. 9 in TYNDALE OLD TESTAMENT COMMENTARY (InterVarsity, 1993).

Historical Background Sources and Handbooks

Bible study becomes more meaningful when modern Western readers understand the times and places in which the biblical authors lived. *The IVP Bible Background Commentary: Old Testament*, by John H. Walton, Victor H. Matthews, and Mark Chavalas (InterVarsity, 2000), provides insight into the ancient Near Eastern world, its peoples, customs, and geography to help contemporary readers better understand the context in which the Old Testament Scriptures were written.

A **handbook** of biblical customs can also be useful. Some good ones are the time-proven updated classic, *Halley's Bible Handbook with the New International Version*, by Henry H. Halley (Zondervan, 2007), and the inexpensive paperback *Manners and Customs in the Bible*, by Victor H. Matthews (Hendrickson, 1991).

Concordances, Dictionaries, and Encyclopedias

A **concordance** lists words of the Bible alphabetically along with each verse in which the word appears. It lets you do your own word studies. An *exhaustive* concordance lists every word used in a given translation, while an *abridged* or *complete* concordance omits either some words, some occurrences of the word, or both.

Two of the best exhaustive concordances are *Strong's Exhaustive Concordance* and *The Strongest NIV Exhaustive Concordance*. Strong's is available based on the King James Version of the Bible and the New American Standard Bible. *Strong's* has an index by which you can find out which Greek or Hebrew word is used in a given English verse. The NIV concordance does the same thing except it also includes an index for Aramaic words in the original texts from which the NIV was translated. However, neither concordance requires knowledge of the original languages. *Strong's* is available online at www.biblestudytools.com. Both are also available in hard copy.

A **Bible dictionary** or **Bible encyclopedia** alphabetically lists articles about people, places, doctrines, important words, customs, and geography of the Bible.

Holman Illustrated Bible Dictionary, by C. Brand, C. W. Draper, and A. England (B&H, 2003), offers more than seven hundred color photos, illustrations, and charts; sixty full-color maps; and up-to-date archeological findings, along with exhaustive definitions of people, places, things, and events—dealing with every subject in the Bible. It uses a variety of Bible translations and is the only dictionary that includes the HCSB, NIV, KJV, RSV, NRSV, REB, NASB, ESV, and TEV.

The New Unger's Bible Dictionary, Revised and Expanded, by Merrill F. Unger (Moody, 2006), has been a best seller for almost fifty years. Its 6,700-plus entries reflect the most current scholarship and more than 1,200,000 words are supplemented with detailed essays, colorful photography and maps, and dozens of charts and illustrations to enhance your understanding of God's Word. Based on the New American Standard Version.

The Zondervan Encyclopedia of the Bible, edited by Moisés Silva and Merrill C. Tenney (Zondervan, 2008), is excellent and exhaustive. However, its five 1,000-page volumes are a financial investment, so all but very serious students may prefer to use it at a church, public, college, or seminary library.

Unlike a Bible dictionary in the above sense, *Vine's Complete Expository Dictionary of Old and New Testament Words*, by W. E. Vine, Merrill F.

Unger, and William White Jr. (Thomas Nelson, 1996), alphabetically lists major words used in the King James Version and defines each Old Testament Hebrew or New Testament Greek word the KJV translates with that English word. *Vine's* lists verse references where that Hebrew or Greek word appears so that you can do your own cross-references and word studies without knowing the original languages.

   The Brown-Driver-Briggs Hebrew and English Lexicon by Francis Brown, C. Briggs, and S. R. Driver (Hendrickson, 1996), is probably the most respected and comprehensive Bible lexicon for Old Testament studies. BDB gives not only dictionary definitions for each word but relates each word to its Old Testament usage and categorizes its nuances of meaning.

Bible Atlases and Map Books

A **Bible atlas** can be a great aid to understanding what is going on in a book of the Bible and how geography affected events. Here are a few good choices:

   The Hammond Atlas of Bible Lands (Langenscheidt, 2007) packs a ton of resources into just sixty-four pages. Maps, of course, but also photographs, illustrations, and a comprehensive timeline. Includes an introduction to the unique geography of the Holy Land, including terrain, trade routes, vegetation, and climate information.

   The New Moody Atlas of the Bible, by Barry J. Beitzel (Moody, 2009), is scholarly, very evangelical, and full of theological text, indexes, and references. Beitzel shows vividly how God prepared the land of Israel perfectly for the acts of salvation He was going to accomplish in it.

   Then and Now Bible Maps Insert (Rose, 2008) is a nifty paperback that is sized just right to fit inside your Bible cover. Only forty-four pages long, it features clear plastic overlays of modern-day cities and countries so you can see what nation or city now occupies the Bible setting you are reading about. Every major city of the Bible is included.

For Small-Group Leaders

Discipleship Journal's Best Small-Group Ideas, Volumes 1 and 2 (NavPress, 2005). Each volume is packed with 101 of the best hands-on tips and group-building principles from *Discipleship Journal's* "Small Group Letter" and "DJ Plus" as well as articles from the magazine. They will help you inject new passion into the life of your small group.

Donahue, Bill. Leading Life-Changing Small Groups (Zondervan, 2002). This comprehensive resource is packed with information, practical tips, and insights that will teach you about small-group philosophy and structure, discipleship, conducting meetings, and more.

McBride, Neal F. *How to Build a Small-Groups Ministry* (NavPress, 1994). *How to Build a Small-Groups Ministry is a time-proven*, hands-on workbook for pastors and lay leaders that includes everything you need to know to develop a plan that fits your unique church. Through basic principles, case studies, and worksheets, McBride leads you through twelve logical steps for organizing and administering a small-groups ministry.

McBride, Neal F. *How to Lead Small Groups* (NavPress, 1990). This book covers leadership skills for all kinds of small groups: Bible study, fellowship, task, and support groups. Filled with step-by-step guidance and practical exercises to help you grasp the critical aspects of small-group leadership and dynamics.

Miller, Tara, and Jenn Peppers. *Finding the Flow: A Guide for Leading Small Groups and Gatherings* (IVP Connect, 2008). Finding the Flow offers a fresh take on leading small groups by seeking to develop the leader's small-group facilitation skills.

Bible Study Methods

Discipleship Journal's Best Bible Study Methods (NavPress, 2002). This is a collection of thirty-two creative ways to explore Scripture that will help you enjoy studying God's Word more.

Hendricks, Howard, and William Hendricks. *Living by the Book: The Art and Science of Reading the Bible* (Moody, 2007). Living by the Book offers a practical three-step process that will help you master simple yet effective inductive methods of observation, interpretation, and application that will make all the difference in your time with God's Word. A workbook by the same title is also available to go along with the book.

The Navigator Bible Studies Handbook (NavPress, 1994). This resource teaches the underlying principles for doing good inductive Bible study, including instructions on doing queston-and-answer studies, verse-analysis studies, chapter-analysis studies, and topical studies.

Warren, Rick. *Rick Warren's Bible Study Methods: Twelve Ways You Can Unlock God's Word* (HarperCollins, 2006). Rick Warren offers simple, step-by-step instructions, guiding you through twelve different approaches to studying the Bible for yourself with the goal of becoming more like Jesus.